Just a Moment

T. D. KEUNE

DEDICATION

To my family, friends and anyone who would take time to savor the moment. Just be in the moment and let that be enough.

ACKNOWLEDGMENTS

In a breath, I would like to thank those who supported, inspired and encouraged me, not only in compiling this collection, but in the course of writing these tiny tomes over a broad swath of time and torment.

T. D. KEUNE

CONTENTS

T. D. KEUNE

JUST A MOMENT
Collected Senryu Poems

T. D. KEUNE

I take a deep breath
The radio plays Pink Floyd
I make my way home

Sleep is my dark foe
A codependent demon
Taunts my waking hours

It is a new day
Wonder and wisdom awaits
Those who seek it out

Listen in sometime
Disregard distracting noise
Find your hidden life

The sun has returned
And the world remains unchanged
What will we do next?

Living is undying
Overcoming all the Hell
That Heaven allows

Don't hop in the back
Enjoy the ride of your life
From the driver's seat

As tough as things get
Who wants to live forever?
One life is enough

What is it you want?
Another expensive toy!
No. No! NO! (sigh) Fine.

Watching and waiting
What is on the other side?
When day becomes night

Many talking heads
Assaulting ears with hot air
Listeners beware!

The heart of the hunt
Balance the need with the want
And find our true home

What is this abuse?
Truth does not bend at the knee
And neither should we

Once more I return
Before the pages unturned
To seek and to learn

A glimmer of hope
Can set the future on fire
Or be extinguished

Old souls and sore toes
Tread tirelessly toward
Their forgotten homes

Be all, be the one
Rise high above the remains
When all comes undone

The trouble with us
Is we think all that we know
Is all that exists

We play this old game
Guided by unspoken rules
No one ever wins

I dream of my youth
That innocent truth I knew
I could never lose

Requesting clearance
To enter your atmosphere
And study your soul

You laugh as I speak
With glee, as a child would be
Proud to be so free

Encapsulated
Individuality
Quietly suppressed

Kingdom of sad clowns
Too proud now to cry out loud
From their weeping stools

Darkness comes faster
When the righteous fail to see
Beyond their own light

Wish away the world
Today, the rest of us will
Stay for tomorrow

Left to wonder how
That bitter flavor, goodbye
Can ever feel right

From the other side
Of the street, I can see you
Watching her watch me

Cavernous echo
To the surface roars a sound
No soul wants around

The only highlight
Of my day, sadly was made
By this blue marker

Pudding pop flashback
Sticky fingers, messy face
Feeling six again

Another meeting
Big cheese has something to share
But none of us care

Gumby was my hero
As a child I wished he would
Defeat my blockheads

My thoughts turn to ink
With each movement of my hand
Creates what I think

A delicate voice
Summons courage to speak words
My heart understood

Gently, so gently
Nudge the timid to the edge
And watch the child fly

I am what you crave
Said the French fry, with a grin
That sly potato!

Puddle before me
Too large to be avoided
So, I leap right in

My lonely orbit
Drawn in by your gravity
Inescapable

Words are the seeds sewn
Deep into the fertile minds
From which stories grow

Particles dancing
Atomic time advancing
Relativity

Lonesome hunger feeds
Upon weaker minds in need
Addicted to greed

Slither silently
Surrender, you sad serpent
Sudden, certain death

DARK SENRYU
31 Horror-inspired Senrya Poems
Celebrating the season of Halloween

T. D. KEUNE

A time of darkness

Night drapes over October

As we welcome fear

Thump! Bumps in the night

Stumble frightened, wander far

Deep into the dark

This realm is too bright

Take me to the darker side

And I shall not hide

From abysmal depths

Comes a tentacled terror

From its ancient keep

Cunning and clever

Sly is the whiskered devil

That crosses your path

The stare from her eyes

Burns like bonfires in the night

Before the witch strikes

Sharp, shrill and steady
Piercing the obsidian
Blood curdling screams

Thickest crimson flows

The belly of what it feeds

Is dark and unknown

Travel not alone

Guided by the scent of fear

Countless teeth draw near

Enter the funhouse

But beware the wicked laugh

Or feel the clown's wrath

Afraid of the dark

But after one night you must

Escape from the light

The last of its kind

Beats rhythmically within

A jar on the shelf

A swing and a hit
Casey did not expect this
Much mess from a corpse

Do not go in there

Stare beyond the blackest void

Awaiting the horde

Long and slow it glides

Darkly drawn through lunar light

And so the moon bleeds

As black as midnight

Patiently poised in the wait

Perched upon the gate

From the soil we come

Silent, we slither closer

As you fall asleep

I am created

A product of mad men's minds

Whom I will not serve

A brief encounter

Emptied of life and reborn

I will bleed no more

The moonlight beckons

At first an itch, then the pain

I prepare to feed

What is this crawling?

Silently creeping along

Many quiet steps

Fragile little thing

Pale and cute, but creepy, too

The doll stares at you

Home alone at night
Eerie silence echoes now
As the lights go out

Repetitive thuds

Against the grain that traps me

And the air depletes

Hiding in plain sight

It waits, it smiles, it follows

Taking its cruel time

Frantic, running teen

He never runs, but keeps up

This is too easy

JUST A MOMENT

T. D. KEUNE

ABOUT THE AUTHOR

T.D. Keune is a partially self-taught artist and writer. He derives much of his work from a love for the movies that began at an early age, fueled as well by an intense curiosity and fascination for all things weird and strange. He was born and raised in rural Missouri, until he relocated to the Saint Louis area, where he resides with his family.

Made in the USA
Las Vegas, NV
25 September 2022

55948413R00052